The Story of
MOVIE STAR
ANNA MAY WONG

The Story of
MOVIE STAR
ANNA MAY WONG

by **Paula Yoo**
with illustrations by **Lin Wang**

Lee & Low Books Inc.
New York

Special thanks to my editors, Jason Low and Jennifer Fox, for their wise editorial advice and guidance.

For Neil Levin—may your star shine brightly forever—P.Y.

For Megan, Nicholas, and Willson—L.W.

Text from *Shining Star: The Anna May Wong Story* copyright © 2009 by Paula Yoo
Sidebar text by Paula Yoo copyright © 2018 by Lee & Low Books Inc.
Illustrations from *Shining Star: The Anna May Wong Story* copyright © 2008 by Lin Wang
p. 15: public domain
p. 17: Photo by Túrelio, used under a Creative Commons Attribution-Share Alike 2.5 Generic License, https://commons.wikimedia.org/wiki/File:Chinatown2_SF.jpg
p. 25: UIG/courtesy Everett Collection
p. 27: public domain
p. 36: Walt Disney Co./courtesy Everett Collection
p. 44: public domain
p. 50: Mary Evans/Ronald Grant/courtesy Everett Collection

LEE & LOW BOOKS Inc., 95 Madison Avenue, New York, NY 10016
leeandlow.com

Manufactured in the United States of America by Lake Book Manufacturing, Inc.
Edited by Jennifer Fox and Kandace Coston
Book design by Neustudio
Book production by The Kids at Our House

The text is set in Vollkorn.
The display font is set in Avenir Next.
The illustrations are rendered in watercolor and acrylic.
10 9 8 7 6 5 4 3 2 1
First Edition
Cataloging-in-Publication data is on file with the Library of Congress.
ISBN 978-1-62014-853-2

TABLE OF CONTENTS

CHAPTER ONE

DREAMS OF STARDOM

Anna May Wong struggled to free herself. Tight ropes bound her to the railroad tracks. A **plume** of smoke puffed into the sky as a train rumbled toward her. . . .

"Stop daydreaming!"

Startled, Anna May opened her eyes. The train vanished. Steam, not smoke, hissed from a nearby boiler filled with dirty clothes.

"Get back to work!" snapped her father. "We have a full day's worth of laundry to clean and press."

Anna May sighed. No longer a **damsel** in distress in an exciting movie, she was just a nine-year-old girl toiling away at her father's laundry in Los Angeles's gritty Chinatown. Her sisters, Mary and Lulu, **scoured** clothes with washing powder against scrub boards. Younger brothers James and Frank squeezed wet trousers through squeaky **cylindrical** dryers. Her mother, with baby Roger strapped to her back, hung up clean dresses to dry on a rod along the ceiling.

Picking up a heavy iron from the coal-burning stove, Anna May felt the familiar ache in her arm. She saw the small burn scars that covered

her hands. She longed to escape this dreary, backbreaking work.

When Anna May finished ironing the shirts, she put them in a basket to lug up the hill to customers' homes. After she completed her deliveries, Anna May counted five pennies in tips. That was enough to buy a movie ticket for the afternoon **matinee!**

There was nothing Anna May enjoyed more than sneaking away to the cinema. Watching a movie, she could escape from her everyday life, travel to interesting places, and experience new things.

Stashing her laundry basket outside, Anna May bought her ticket and slipped into the theater. Everyone gasped when the **heroine** of the movie was trapped in a sawmill. Anna May covered her eyes and peeked between her fingers. The heroine, with her hands and feet tied, lay on a moving **conveyor belt** headed toward the huge, spinning blades. . . .

Suddenly lights flooded the room. The movie had ended with a cliff-hanger. Anna May would have to wait until the following week to see if the heroine would be rescued.

Anna May wished life was like the movies. She dreamed of a hero coming along to rescue her from working in the laundry, and from the bullies at school.

Most of the boys and girls at Anna May's school were white. They taunted Anna May, yanking her pigtails and shouting "Chinaman" and other hurtful names. Her father told Anna May to stay quiet and not fight back. "Hold no **malice** in your heart toward anyone," he said. "We must be proud always of our people and race."

Anna May tried hard to follow her father's advice, but still she hated going to school. One morning as Anna May reluctantly dragged herself to school, she noticed a police **barricade** on Flower Street. Giant cameras and lights filled the sidewalk. A man aimed a camera at a woman dressed in rags. They were filming a movie!

During the next few weeks, the movie set became Anna May's new classroom. She regularly skipped school to watch the action on the set and ask questions about filmmaking. The amused actors and crew soon gave Anna May a nickname—the Curious Chinese Child.

Anna May loved this exciting world and wanted to be part of it. She decided she would become an actress. Instead of watching movies, she would star in them. She would be rich and famous so she could support her family. No one would ever have to work in the laundry again.

America's Chinatowns

When Chinese immigrants first moved to San Francisco in the 1800s, discrimination prohibited them from living in certain parts of the city. As a result, most immigrants ended up settling in the same neighborhood near the East Bay. They called this area *"Dai Fou,"* which means "Big City."

By 1848, *Dai Fou* became known as the country's first and oldest "Chinatown." It was the economic, cultural, and political center for Chinese immigrants who missed their families and homes in China. Many immigrants settled in boarding houses, which provided a room and regular meals. They also served as community centers where people could **socialize,** and provided an address immigrants could use to send or receive mail from their families in China. As Chinatown's population grew, so did its businesses. Many Chinese immigrants set up restaurants, food markets, stores, and laundries in the neighborhood.

As Chinese people moved throughout the United States, pursuing jobs and other economic opportunities, similar Chinatowns were created in cities

Dupont Street, now called Grant Avenue, in
Chinatown, San Francisco, 1910.

across the country, including New York, Chicago, Boston, Philadelphia, St. Louis, Minneapolis, and Butte, Montana. The Chinatown in Los Angeles, where Anna May Wong grew up, was established in 1880 and included restaurants, shops, laundries, and low-income housing for immigrant families. By 1910, it had expanded to over 15 streets and 200 buildings, complete with a Chinese opera theatre and three temples.

During the 1920s and 1930s, movie-making boomed in Los Angeles, and many movies were filmed in Chinatown. Today, approximately 15,907 people live in Los Angeles's Chinatown area. But unlike during Anna May Wong's time, the population is now very diverse. Asian, Latinx, African American, and white people all live together in Chinatown.

Grant Avenue in Chinatown, San Francisco, 2012.

CHAPTER 2

ANNA THE ACTRESS

Every day, Anna May would rush home to **reenact** the scenes from the film in her bedroom. She practiced different emotions in front of her mirror. For fear, she gasped and collapsed to the floor. For anger, she snarled and curled her fingers into claws.

One evening Anna May's parents caught her weeping at the mirror, dabbing her eyes with a handkerchief. She confessed she was imitating

the actors she watched at a movie set instead of attending school. Furious, her father shouted, "You have to go to school! Not play hooky!" Actresses were looked down upon in traditional Chinese society, he said. "A good girl will not be an actress."

Anna May's father punished her, forbidding her from cutting school again. But no punishment could discourage Anna May from her dreams of stardom. Throughout her school years, she secretly visited movie sets whenever she had the chance.

When Anna May was a teenager, her father got her a job as a secretary. He hoped lining up a steady career for her after high school would end her Hollywood fantasies. Instead, Anna May was fired after only one week because of her poor **shorthand** skills.

Anna May grew to a height of five feet seven inches and she dressed in the latest 1920s "flapper" fashions. She cut her hair into a stylish bob with blunt bangs. She was beautiful and had many admirers. One was a movie director who needed three hundred Chinese men and women to work as extras in his film *The Red Lantern*. Anna May begged her father to let her **audition** for a part. She could earn seven dollars and fifty cents each day. Her father **grudgingly** gave his permission because their family needed the money.

Anna May was chosen as an extra for the movie. On her first day of shooting, hoping to look like a star, she dusted her face with rice powder. She curled her hair and rubbed several wet sheets of red-dyed Chinese tissue paper over her lips and cheeks. To her embarrassment, the director laughed and made her wash her face. Anna May was disappointed to discover her job was very simple. All she had to do was carry a red lantern down the street.

Over the next few years, Anna May worked as an extra in many movies, hoping one day to be discovered and offered a bigger role. She never complained about the long hours on sets, and she followed all the directors' orders. Soon movie critics were **praising** her large, expressive eyes and ability to convey emotion with graceful hand movements.

Although Anna May's father still disapproved of her career as an actress, he admired her **diligence**. If he couldn't change her stubborn mind about Hollywood, he explained to his daughter, then he would do his best to help her succeed. Anna May's father insisted on driving her to all her auditions. He also suggested that she live at home. Instead of paying rent for an apartment, she could save her hard-earned money.

The Rise of Hollywood

Today, when people hear the word "Hollywood," they think of movies, celebrities, and glamour. But in 1870, Hollywood was a small neighborhood in Los Angeles, California. It had one post office, one hotel, and two grocery markets. It didn't become known for film-making until the early 1900s, when several movie companies moved west and set up production in the area. California offered more advantages for filmmakers than the East Coast, including year-round **temperate** and mostly sunny weather, diverse geography for outdoor film shoots, and cheap real estate. Los Angeles also provided affordable labor since labor unions—organizations that protect the rights and further the interests of workers—had not yet been established there.

During the 1920s, many more film companies moved to the Hollywood area, including Paramount, Warner Bros., RKO, and Columbia. Movies were becoming more popular, so to better showcase them, movie theaters, also called "picture palaces," were built so that a large audience could watch a movie at the same time. The Roxy Theatre in New York City

The original Hollywood sign, constructed in 1923. The last four letters were removed when the sign was restored in 1949.

could accommodate 6,200 people at once! Because the technology to **synchronize** film with sound did not exist yet, movies were shown with "intertitles" so the audience could read the dialogue. An orchestra or a solo pianist or organist would provide live music to enhance the movie's emotional appeal.

Movies back then were filmed on long strips of celluloid, a transparent plastic, which were wrapped around large metal reels. A thousand feet of celluloid equaled about fifteen minutes of a movie, and a movie's length was measured by the number of reels it required. Advancements in technology soon led to the "feature film"—a movie that could last for an hour. Films would be packaged with a news broadcast, called a "newsreel"; an animated cartoon; advertisements; and other short movies of various kinds. One fifteen-cent admission in 1927 could get you a whole afternoon of entertainment!

The year 1927 saw the release of the first movie to include sound, *The Jazz Singer.* The movie featured speech, singing, and music that were recorded separately, then synchronized with the movie's events. As films with sound, also called "talkies," grew in popularity, studios had to make many changes to incorporate sound into their feature films. Capturing sound required special equipment and engineers who knew how to use it, which made production costly. Actors had to learn their lines before they filmed their scenes so that both visuals and sound could be recorded at the same time. The technology for microphones improved to make them more sensitive to sounds, but this meant that

Poster of the 1927 film *The Jazz Singer*.

background noises could interfere with sound quality. Filmmakers had to find quiet, controlled places where they could make their movies.

The addition of sound also changed how movies

were displayed and how audiences experienced them. Projectionists who operated the film reels that supplied the movie's visuals were now also responsible for working phonographs that provided the movie's sound. If the sound fell out of sync with the picture, the audience would cause a **ruckus** until the projectionist fixed it. Without the help of intertitles, theatergoers had to keep quiet to hear the actors' dialogue and follow the storyline. The addition of sound to film revolutionized the movie-making industry, and for actresses like Anna May Wong, who could now be seen *and* heard, it dramatically increased their fame and popularity.

CHAPTER THREE

A RISING STAR

Anna May won her first big role in *Bits of Life,* a 1921 movie starring Lon Chaney as a Chinese man named Chin Chow. She played his wife, Toy Sing. To her shock, Anna May learned they were not allowed to kiss on-screen. Movie studios **forbade** actors and actresses of color to kiss their white costars because they feared audiences would disapprove.

Even worse, Anna May saw a makeup artist dusting yellow powder on Chaney's face to give him what they claimed was Chinese skin coloring. He also used tape and **spirit gum** to pull Chaney's eyes into an exaggerated slant. This makeup was called "yellowface."

The yellowface makeup disturbed Anna May. Her father had always told her to be proud of her race, but the ugly makeup made her feel ashamed. She wondered if movie viewers would assume all Chinese people looked that horrible.

Still, Anna May was earning one hundred and fifty dollars a week, money her family needed. She put her concerns aside and played the role.

In her next several films, Anna May won small supporting parts. Although she was proud to help her family with her earnings from these movies, she wasn't proud of the roles. Many of her characters portrayed Chinese women in a negative light and

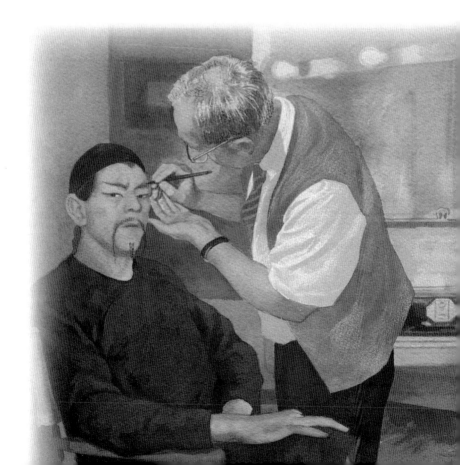

promoted **stereotypes**—from the scared and submissive "China doll" to the evil and **domineering** "dragon lady."

Anna May hated these **demeaning** images, but she could not afford to turn down the parts. Still, she always gave her best performance, hoping one day to play a **dignified** leading role. Frustrated with the roles in Hollywood, Anna May moved to Europe for a few years and won

supporting parts in British and German films. In 1929, her role as a graceful dancer in *Piccadilly* made her an overnight sensation in Europe. People mobbed her everywhere she went, and European girls cut their bangs short like hers. She had finally achieved her dream of international movie stardom.

CHAPTER FOUR
BROKEN DREAMS

A confident Anna May returned to the United States in 1935 to audition for what was considered the most important movie of its time for Asian American actors. The film version of Pearl S. Buck's Pulitzer Prize-winning novel, *The Good Earth,* would depict China in a realistic manner.

Anna May wanted the lead role of O-lan, the loyal and kindhearted wife to Chinese farmer Wang Lung. But the role of Wang Lung had already been given to Austrian-born actor Paul Muni. In the script, O-lan had to kiss her husband. Because of the movie studio rule against interracial kissing, only a white actress could be cast as his wife. German-born actress Luise Rainer won the role.

Heartbroken, Anna May stood at a crossroad in her career. Her ethnicity was keeping her from achieving her dream of becoming a Hollywood star. She loved acting but was uncomfortable taking roles that presented racist images. She wondered why Hollywood and Americans accepted these unfair views. Was she doing more harm than good with these movie parts? "I'm torn between my race and my American homeland," she said.

Not feeling welcome in her own country anymore, Anna May decided to go to China. She would visit her parents, who had recently retired and moved back there. Although Anna May had

never been to China, she was eager to learn more about her heritage. "I'm traveling to a strange country," she told reporters as she boarded the SS *President Hoover*. "And yet, in a way, I am going home."

Whitewashing

The term "whitewashing" describes what happens when a white actor is cast in a role for a character originally written or **conceived** to be non-white. This casting practice has been done for decades in Hollywood. The term became popular again in recent years when Asian American activists protested the whitewashing of Asian and Asian American roles in Hollywood movies. Recent movies criticized for whitewashing include the 2017 version of the popular Japanese manga and anime series *Ghost in the Shell*, which cast Scarlett Johansson as its Japanese main character; and *Doctor Strange*, which cast Tilda Swinton as "The Ancient One."

Tilda Swinton and Chiwetel Ejiofor in *Doctor Strange*, 2016.

Critics say that this whitewashing trend erases or **trivializes** the presence of people of color in the media. There are even movies where an Asian character is simply rewritten to be a white person. For example, the movie *21* was based on the real life of Eugene Ma, an Asian American MIT student who used his math skills to win big at casinos in Las Vegas. The character was rewritten to be a white male MIT student instead and the movie featured a white American actor portraying a fictional character based on Ma.

Many activists also criticize Hollywood movies and TV shows that focus on a story set in Asian and/or Asian American culture but are told from the point of view of an "outsider" white character living in that world. Examples range from *The Last Samurai* to *The Great Wall* to the TV series *Iron Fist*.

The situation in Hollywood seems to be improving as more actors become aware of the controversy. When actor Ed Skrein was cast to play the role of the Asian character Major Ben Daimio in the 2019 movie *Hellboy*, the Asian American community protested the whitewashing on social media. Skrein decided to turn down the role in order for an Asian American actor to be cast instead, stating, "Representation of ethnic diversity is important, especially to me as I have a mixed heritage family. It is our responsibility to make moral decisions in difficult times and to give voice to inclusivity. It is my hope that one day these discussions will become less necessary and that we can help make equal representation in the Arts a reality." As a result, Asian American actor Daniel Dae Kim was cast in the role.

A 2018 Motion Picture Association of America survey reported that Latinxs and Asian Americans dominated movie audiences in 2017. As the number of minorities in the US continues to increase, especially at the movies, it appears Hollywood has taken notice. In 2018 the film *Crazy Rich Asians* became the first major studio movie featuring an all-Asian cast in 25 years. It grossed over $110 million in the US within its first three weeks of opening. With more and more people from diverse backgrounds demanding to be authentically reflected on-screen, it will be interesting to see how moviemakers and moviegoers continue to shape the future of Hollywood.

CHAPTER FIVE
ANNA IN CHINA

Anna May arrived in Shanghai on February 9, 1936. Along with the thousands of cheering Chinese fans waiting for her at the pier were just as many Chinese people who resented her for playing movie roles they believed were disrespectful to Asians. A gracious Anna May defended her career, saying that if she was to be an actress, she often had no choice when it came to the parts she could play.

During her stay, Anna May absorbed as much

Chinese culture as she could. She studied Chinese **philosophy,** attended a Chinese drama school, and took Chinese language classes. She went to fancy fifteen-course meals with **ambassadors** to help create goodwill between China and the United States. At a silk factory, Anna May was fitted for a traditional silk dress called a *cheongsam* to show her pride in her Chinese heritage. She also rode rickshaws, visited temples, saw the Great Wall of China, and signed autographs for eager Chinese fans.

In her family's ancestral village of Chang On, Anna May and her father talked for hours on the steps of his house. For the first time he opened up to her about his childhood in Sacramento, California, where he had worked in dangerous gold mines. She learned how much her father had sacrificed so their family could have a better life in America. Then he reminded her, "We must be proud always of our people and race."

Anna May understood her father better and felt proud of his accomplishments. As she gazed into her father's eyes, she realized he was proud of her too. Anna May decided that she would honor her father and her Chinese heritage by fighting for more **authentic** images of Asians on-screen. "I will never play again in a film which shows the Chinese in an **unsympathetic** light," she vowed.

Anna May Wong looked forward to her future in Hollywood, playing parts she could be proud of. And for the first time in her life, she truly felt like a shining star.

The Chinese in America

It all began with Gold Mountain.

By the 19th century, China had fallen from one of the most powerful nations in the world to one of the poorest. Its population had doubled from 150 million in the year 1650 to 300 million by 1800. There were not enough jobs available for everyone or enough farmland available to grow crops to feed people.

Across the Pacific Ocean, a miner named James W. Marshall discovered gold at Sutter's Mill in Coloma, California, in 1848. This led to the **California Gold Rush**, as people from all over the US moved to California in hopes of finding gold. The news soon spread as far away as China. The Chinese called America *"Gum Shan,"* which meant "Gold Mountain." Thousands of men left China for America in hopes of striking it rich for their families.

When these immigrants arrived, they did not find gold. Instead, many of them were forced to take on physically difficult jobs for very little pay. Some immigrants worked in the gold mines belonging to white settlers. More helped create the **transcontinental**

43

THE ONLY ONE BARRED OUT.

ENLIGHTENED AMERICAN STATESMAN.—"We must draw the line *somewhere*, you know."

A political cartoon from 1881, showing a Chinese man being barred entry to the "Golden Gate of Liberty."

railroad, which linked the west coast of the US to the existing eastern rail network. They risked their lives every day with these dangerous jobs. In addition, many

Chinese immigrants worked as domestic servants, housekeepers, and farmers. Others started their own restaurants, stores, and laundries. The laundry business became one of the more popular jobs for Chinese immigrants; by 1900, one in four men worked in a laundry, including Anna May Wong's father.

The Chinese population in America exploded from 4,000 in the year 1850 to over 100,000 by 1880. This increase stirred anti-Chinese feelings within the white American population, who feared losing their jobs to the immigrants. Anti-Chinese sentiments led to acts of racism and violence towards Chinese people living on the west coast. Many were driven from their settlements by shows of **animosity** or legislation like the **Chinese Exclusion Act** (1882), which restricted Chinese laborers from immigrating to the United States. It was the first US law to limit immigration to America on the basis of a person's race. Not until 1943, when the United States and China formed an alliance during World War II, did the US government allow Chinese immigrants to move to America again. In 1965, the **Immigration and Nationality Act** removed limits on the number of Asian immigrants entering the US.

Today, there are almost 328 million people living in America. Out of that number, nearly four million are of Chinese descent. According to the latest United States Census Bureau statistics, the Asian population in the US is growing the fastest of all racial groups. Researchers predict that people of Asian descent will jump from 5.4% of the US population to 9.3% by 2060.

CHAPTER SIX
THE COMEBACK

Anna May kept her word. After returning to Hollywood, her first of many positive roles was in *Daughter of Shanghai,* released in 1937. She played a loyal, loving Chinese American daughter who solves the mystery of her father's murder. "I like my part in this picture better than any I've had before," she said proudly. "This picture gives

the Chinese a break—we have sympathetic parts for a change. To me that means a great deal."

For the rest of her acting career, Anna May Wong accepted only positive roles, including the characters of Lin Ying in *Bombs Over Burma* (1943) and Kwan Mei in *The Lady from Chungking* (1942). Anna May donated money she earned from these movies to the China War Relief to aid Chinese refugees during the Japanese invasions of the late 1930s. She also auctioned off her **extensive** collection of ball gowns and sent the money and medical supplies to China during World War II.

In the 1950s, Anna May made the transition from movies to television, starring in guest roles on popular shows such as *The Life and Legend of Wyatt Earp* and the Mike Hammer detective series. She also starred in a short-lived TV show called *The Gallery of Madame Liu-Tsong,* about an art gallery owner/detective who hunted for art treasures. *Portrait in Black,* the last of more than fifty films in which Anna May appeared, was released in 1960.

Anna May never married or had children. In

her later years, she lived with her brother Richard and owned several cats and dogs. She also carefully tended a large garden of exotic plants.

On February 3, 1961, Anna May Wong died in her sleep of a heart attack at the age of fifty-six. For many years after her death, her career was viewed in a negative light. Film scholars and the general public criticized what they perceived to be her stereotypical portrayals of Asian characters.

In recent years, however, many scholars and fans have realized how much Anna May struggled in her fight against discrimination in the movie industry. Critics now praise Anna May's ability to portray her limited roles with humanity and sympathy. Today, aspiring Asian American actors and actresses acknowledge her important contributions to improving Asian images on-screen. Anna May Wong said she felt "suspended between worlds" because of her Chinese ancestry and American upbringing. Her legacy bridged a gap between both worlds and helped open doors for today's generation of actors.

TIMELINE

1905 January 3: Anna May Wong is born in Los Angeles, California

1921 Performed her first big role in *Bits of Life*

1928 Frustrated with the roles Hollywood offered, Anna moved to Europe to pursue other acting opportunities

1929 Became an overnight sensation for her role in *Piccadilly*

1935 Returned to the United States hoping to play a major role in *The Good Earth*

1936 February 9: Traveled to Shanghai, China, to visit her parents

1937 Returned to Hollywood for *Daughter of Shanghai,* her first positive and authentic role

1950s Transitioned from film to TV

1960 Gave final performance in the movie *Portrait in Black*

1961 February 3: Died at the age of 56

GLOSSARY

ambassador (am-BAS-ah-door) *noun* a high-ranking government official who represents their country within the territory of a different country

animosity (an-eh-MAH-seh-tee) *noun* a feeling of intense dislike

audition (aww-DEH-shun) *noun* a short presentation a performer gives to show off their talents to be considered for a role or part in a production

authentic (aw-THEN-tik) *adjective* genuine

barricade (BARE-eh-kade) *noun* a non-permanent structure built to block an entrance or area

California Gold Rush (KA-leh-FOR-nyeh gold rush) *proper noun* a historical event that lasted from 1848-1855. After gold was found in Coloma, California, 300,000 people from across the US and around the world came to the area in the hopes of finding gold and becoming wealthy

Chinese Exclusion Act (CHI-nees eks-KLOO-shun akt) *proper noun* a federal law signed in the year 1882 that prohibited Chinese workers from immigrating to the US. It was the first major act of legislation to restrict immigration to the US

conceive (KON-seev) *verb* to create or imagine

conveyor belt (kon-VAY-er BELT) *noun* a long stretch of material that moves continuously to carry objects from place to place

cylindrical (sil-IN-drik-al) *adjective* a three-sided object with straight sides and circular ends. A soda can is an example of a cylinder

damsel (DAM-zel) *noun* a young unmarried lady

demeaning (dee-MEAN-ing) *adjective* less worthy of respect

diligence (DILL-eh-jence) *noun* focus

dignified (DIG-nif-eyed) *adjective* showing dignity or self-respect

domineering (DOM-in-EAR-ring) *adjective* controlling or intimidating

ethnicity (eth-NEH-seh-tee) *noun* a large group of people who share the same customs, religious practices, or background

extensive (ex-TEN-siv) *adjective* large

forbade (FOR-bade) *verb* the past tense of forbid, to command someone not to do something

grudgingly (GRUD-jing-lee) *adverb* to do something unwillingly

heroine (HEER-oh-in) *noun* a woman who is admired for her courage and other noble qualities

Immigration and Nationality Act (EM-mi-GRAY-shun and NASH-un-al-it-tee akt) *proper noun* federal legislation signed in 1965 that made it illegal to prohibit a person from immigrating to the US on the basis of their race, ancestry, or nation of origin

malice (MAL-is) *noun* a feeling of wanting to cause harm to someone else

matinee (MAT-in-nay) *noun* a movie or play performed in the afternoon

reenact (REE-in-act) *verb* to repeat an action or event

philosophy (fill-AH-so-fee) *noun* the study of knowledge and ideas about the meaning of life

plume (ploom) *noun* the shape of steam, smoke, or water as it rises into the air

ruckus (RUK-kus) *noun* a noisy commotion

scoured (SCOW-erd) *verb* to clean by rubbing something hard against a rough surface

shorthand (SHORT-hand) *noun* a way of writing quickly that uses abbreviations in place of words or phrases

socialize (SO-she-lize) *verb* to speak or interact with other people in a casual way

spirit gum (SPEER-it gum) *noun* a fast-drying solution that actors use to attach fake hair and other accessories to their faces

stereotypes (STARE-ee-oh-TYPES) *noun* false beliefs that a great number of people may have about all people with a specific characteristic

synchronize (SYN-kro-nize) *verb* to make two or more things happen at the same time or speed

temperate (TEM-purr-eht) *adjective* having weather with temperatures that are not too hot or too cold

transcontinental railroad (trans-KON-tin-en-tul RAIL-road) *noun* a railroad system built between 1863 and 1869 that connected the East and West coasts of the US, formally known as the First Transcontinental Railroad

trivialize (TREV-ee-ah-lize) *verb* to make something seem less important than it is

unsympathetic (UN-SIM-pah-theh-tick) *adjective* uncaring or insensitive

TEXT SOURCES

Chan, Anthony B. *Perpetually Cool: The Many Lives of Anna May Wong (1905-1961)*, Lanham, MD: Rowan & Littlefield, Scarecrow Press, 2003.

Chang, Iris. *The Chinese in America: A Narrative History.* New York: Penguin Books, 2004.

Hodges, Graham Russell Gao. *Anna May Wong: From Laundryman's Daughter to Hollywood Legend.* New York: Palgrave Macmillan, 2004.

Leibfried, Philip, and Chei Mi Lane. *Anna May Wong: A Complete Guide to Her Film, Stage, Radio and Television Work.* Jefferson, NC: McFarland & Company, Inc., 2004.

Leong, Karen J. *The China Mystique: Pearl S. Buck, Anna May Wong, Mayling Soong, and the Transformation of American Orientalism.* Berkeley: University of California Press, 2005.

SIDEBAR SOURCES

AMERICA'S CHINATOWNS

Chinese Historical Society of Southern California. "Chinese in America." Accessed May 14, 2018. http://www.chssc.org/History/Timeline.aspx (link discontinued)

Goyette, Braden. "How Racism Created America's Chinatowns." Accessed May 14, 2018. https://www.huffingtonpost.com/2014/11/11/american-chinatowns-history_n_6090692.html

Tsui, Bonnie. *American Chinatown: A People's History of Five Neighborhoods.* New York: Simon & Schuster, Inc., 2009.

THE RISE OF HOLLYWOOD

AMC Film Site. "The History of Film: The 1920s, The Pre-Talkies and the Silent Era." Accessed May 14, 2018. http://www.filmsite.org/20sintro.html

Foster, Diana. "The History of Silent Movies and Subtitles." Posted November 19, 2014. https://www.octaneseating.com/history-of-silent-movies

Roland, Zelda. "How Did Hollywood End Up in . . . Hollywood?" Accessed May 14, 2018. https://www.kcet.org/shows/lost-la/how-did-hollywood-end-up-in-hollywood

Schatz, Thomas. *Boom and Bust: American Cinema in the 1940s*. History of the American Cinema. Berkeley: University of California Press, 1999.

Thompson, Emily. "A Very Short History of the Transition from Silent to Sound Movies." Accessed June 14, 2018. http://www.wonderstruckthebook.com/essay_silent-to-sound.htm

WHITEWASHING

Brevet, Brad. "'Crazy Rich Asians' Tops Labor Day Weekend, 'Fallout' is Big in China & 'Incredibles 2' Tops $600 million." Box Office Mojo. Posted September 2, 2018. https://www.boxofficemojo.com/news/?id=4433&p=.htm

Couch, Aaron and Borys Kit. "Ed Skrein Exits 'Hellboy' Reboot After Whitewashing Outcry." *Hollywood Reporter,* August 28, 2017. https://www.hollywoodreporter.com/heat-vision/ed-skrein-exits-hellboy-reboot-whitewashing-outcry-1033431

Locker, Melissa. "Latinos and Asians Dominated Movie Audiences in 2017. Will Hollywood Listen?" *Fast Company*, April 5, 2018. https://www.fastcompany.com/40554898/latinos-and-asians-dominated-movie-audiences-in-2017-will-hollywood-listen

Lowe, Kenneth. "The Scrutable West: Industry Bias, Whitewashing and the Invisible Asian in Hollywood." *Paste Magazine,* September 16, 2017. https://www.pastemagazine.com/articles/2017/09/bias-does-not-come-out-with-the-whitewash.html

Motion Picture Association of America. "Theme Report: A comprehensive analysis and survey of the theatrical and home entertainment market environment (THEME) for 2017." Accessed May 14, 2018. https://www.mpaa.org/wp-content/uploads/2018/04/MPAA-THEME-Report-2017_Final.pdf

Scherker, Amanda. "Whitewashing Was One Of Hollywood's Worst Habits. So Why Is It Still Happening?" *Huffington Post*, last updated December 6, 2017. https://www.huffingtonpost.com/2014/07/10/hollywood-whitewashing_n_5515919.html

United States Census Bureau. Accessed March 23, 2018. https://www.census.gov

THE CHINESE IN AMERICA

Asia for Educators. "Introduction to China's Modern History." Accessed May 14, 2018. http://afe.easia.columbia.edu/timelines/china_modern_timeline.htm

Brands, H. W. *The Age of Gold: the California Gold Rush and the New American Dream.* New York: Anchor Books, 2002.

Chin, Doug. "The Chinese Exclusion Acts: A Racist Chapter in U.S. Civil Rights History." Accessed May 14, 2018. http://ocaseattle.org/2012/05/21/the-chinese-exclusion-acts-a-racist-chapter-in-u-s-civil-rights-history/

Lee, Erika. *The Making of Asian America: A History.* New York: Simon & Schuster, 2015.

Smith-Baranzin, Marlene. *A Golden State: Mining and Economic Development in Gold Rush California.* Berkeley: University of California Press, 1999.

United States Census Bureau. Accessed May 14, 2018. https://www.census.gov

RECOMMENDED FURTHER READING

Fiction books are marked with an asterisk.

EARLY FILMMAKING AND PERFORMERS

Malone, Alicia. *Backwards and in Heels: The Past, Present and Future of Women Working in Film.* Miami, FL: Mango, 2018.

Mochizuki, Ken. *Be Water, My Friend: The Early Years of Bruce Lee.* New York: Lee & Low Books, 2006.

* Selznick, Brian. *The Invention of Hugo Cabret.* New York: Scholastic, 2007.

* Selznick, Brian. *Wonderstruck.* New York: Scholastic, 2011.

CHINESE IMMIGRATION

* Honeyman, Kay. *The Fire Horse Girl.* New York: Arthur A. Levine Books/Scholastic, 2013.

* Russell, Ching Yeung. *Tofu Quilt.* New York: Lee & Low Books, 2009.

Wilson, Steve. *The California Gold Rush: Chinese Laborers in America (1848-1882).* New York: PowerKids Press/Rosen Publishing, 2016.

* Yep, Laurence. *Dragonwings.* New York: Harper & Row, 1975.

SELECTED MOVIES AND VIDEOS

Piccadilly (1929)

A Study in Scarlet (1933)

Daughter of Shanghai (1937)

Lady from Chungking (1942)

"*Dangerous to Know: The Career and Legacy of Anna May Wong.*" Excerpts from a panel held at the Castro Theatre. (February 27, 2004) https://www.youtube.com/watch?v=Uv-Lo6s7M3Q

ABOUT THE AUTHOR AND ILLUSTRATOR

PAULA YOO is an author and screenwriter whose children's books for Lee & Low include *Sixteen Years in Sixteen Seconds, Shining Star,* and several titles in the Confetti Kids series. Her titles have been recognized by the International Reading Association, the Texas Bluebonnet Award Master List, and Lee & Low's New Voices Award. She and her husband live in Los Angeles, California, where she works in television. You can visit her online at paulayoo.com.

LIN WANG has illustrated several books for children, including *The Crane Girl* for Lee & Low Books. She is a classically trained portrait painter with an MFA from the Savannah College of Art and Design, and her work has been recognized by the Society of Illustrators Original Art Show. Wang lives in the San Francisco Bay Area with her husband and their children.